Impressum
Verlag: BABADADA GmbH, Nedderfeld 112 , 22529 Hamburg
Geschäftsführer / Verlagsleitung: Harald Hof
Druck: Books on Demand GmbH, In de Tarpen 42, 22848 Norderstedt

Imprint
Publisher: BABADADA GmbH, Nedderfeld 112 , 22529 Hamburg, Germany
Managing Director / Publishing direction: Harald Hof
Print: Books on Demand GmbH, In de Tarpen 42, 22848 Norderstedt

school

scol

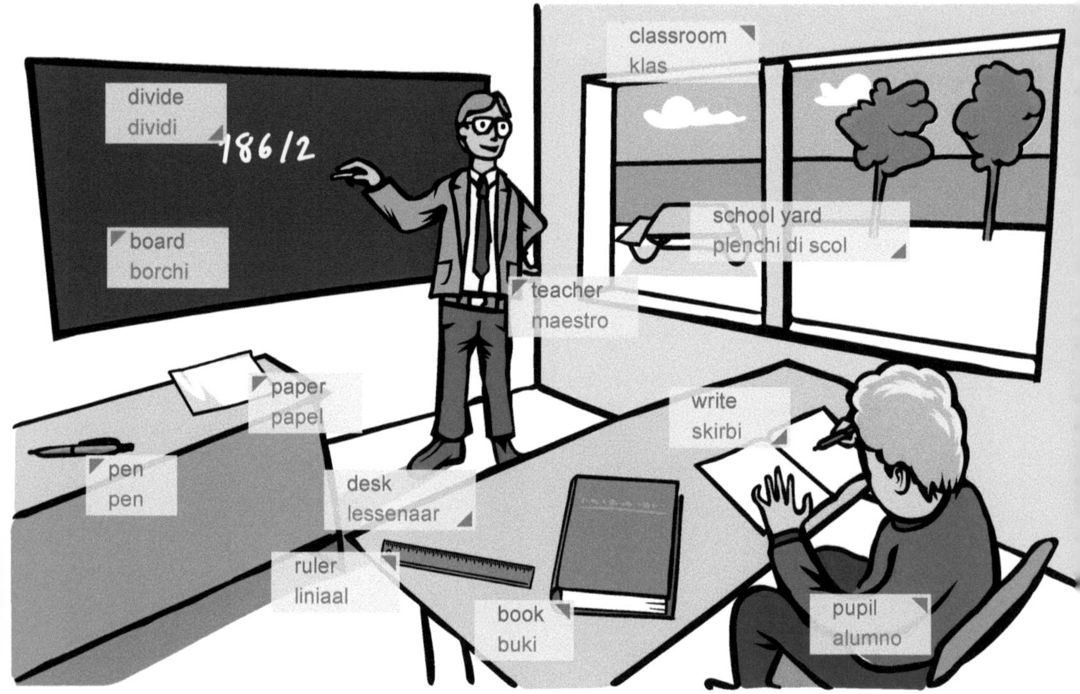

classroom
klas
divide
dividi
186/2
board
borchi
teacher
maestro
school yard
plenchi di scol
paper
papel
write
skirbi
pen
pen
desk
lessenaar
ruler
liniaal
book
buki
pupil
alumno

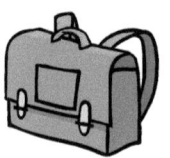

satchel

tas di scol

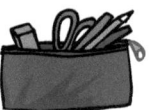

pencil case

etui

pencil

potlood

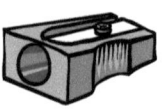

pencil sharpener

slijper

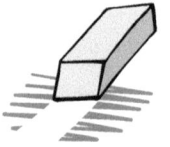

rubber

gum

drawing pad

buki di pinta

drawing

pintura

paintbrush

cuashi

paint box

caha di verf

scissors

sker

glue

lijm

exercise book

schrift

homework

huiswerk

12

number

number

2+2

add

suma

5-2

subtract

kita

2×2

multiply

multiplica

calculate

conta

A

letter

letter

ABCDEFG
HIJKLMN
OPQRSTU
VWXYZ

alphabet

alfabet

word

palabra

text
texto

read
lesa

chalk
krijt

lesson
les

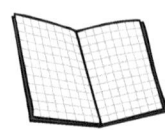

register
klassenboek

exam
examen

certificate
diploma

school uniform
uniform di scol

education
estudio

encyclopedia
enciclopedia

university
universidad

microscope
microscop

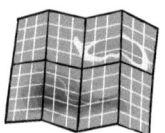

map
mapa

waste-paper basket
bari di sushi

school - scol

hotel
hotel

Grand

hostel
posada

ROOMS

bureau de change
oficina di cambio

CHANGE

car
auto

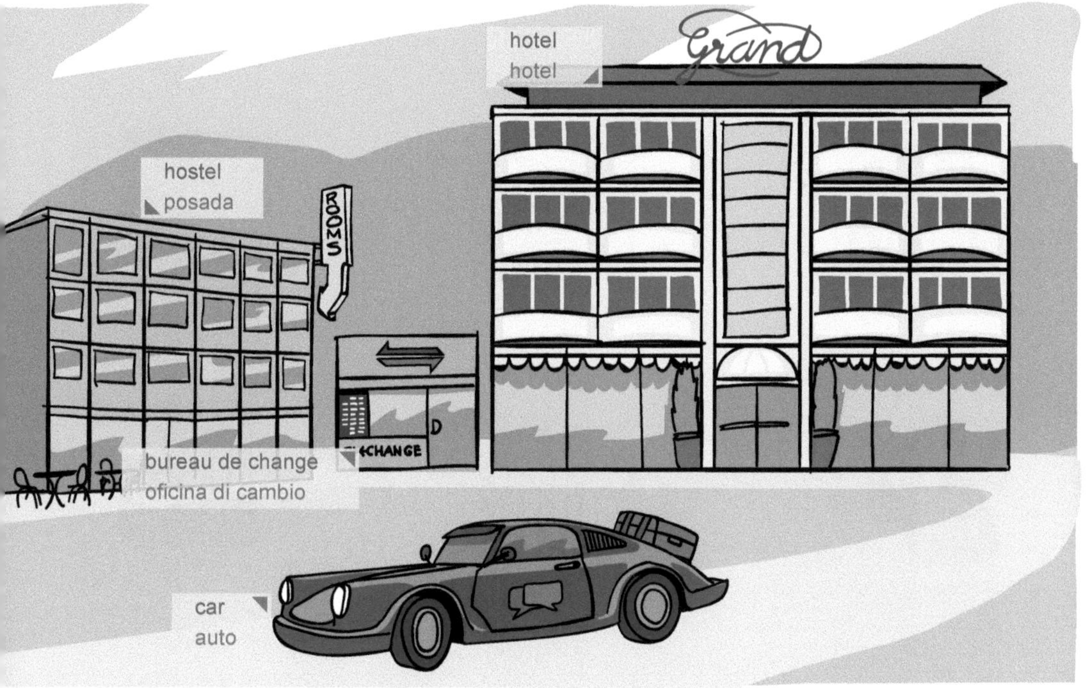

language

idioma

yes / no

si / no

Okay

bon

hello

hallo

translator

tolk

Thank you

masha danki

how much is...?

Cuanto esaki ta costa?

I do not understand

Mi no ta compronde

problem

problema

Good evening!

bon nochi

Good morning!

Bon dia!

Good night!

Bon nochi!

bye bye

ayo

direction

direccion

luggage

maleta

bag

handbag

backpack

rugtas

guest

huesped

room

camber

sleeping bag

slaapzak

tent

tent

travel - biahamento

tourist information

informacion pa turista

beach

lama

credit card

credit card

breakfast

desayuno

lunch

cuminda di merdia

dinner

cuminda di anochi

ticket

carchi

lift

cabe'i boto

stamp

stampia

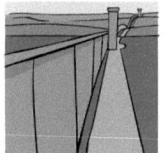

border

grens

customs

duana

embassy

embahada

visa

visa

passport

paspoort

transport
transport

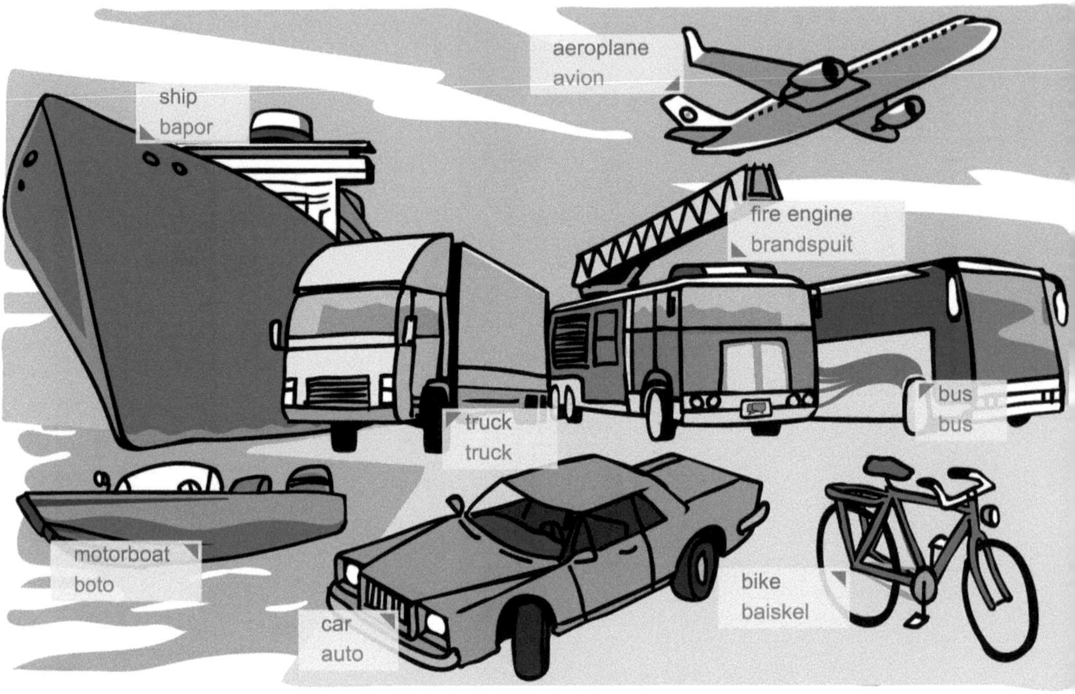
aeroplane
avion
ship
bapor
fire engine
brandspuit
bus
bus
truck
truck
motorboat
boto
bike
baiskel
car
auto

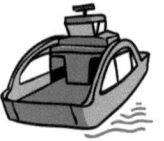

ferry
ferry

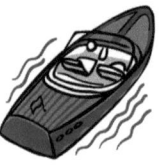

boat
boto

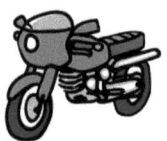

motorbike
brommer

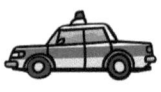

police car
auto di polis

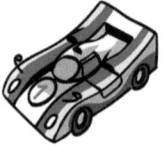

racing car
auto di careda

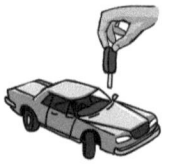

rental car
auto di huur

car sharing

car sharing

breakdown truck

takelwagen

refuse truck

dump truck

motor

motor

fuel

gasolin

petrol station

pomp di gasolin

traffic sign

borchi di trafico

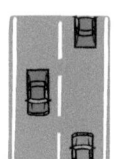

traffic

trafico

traffic jam

fila

car park

parkeerplaats

train station

stacion di trein

tracks

riel

train

trein

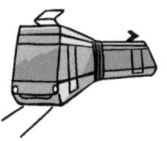

tram

tram

carriage

wagon

helicopter

helicopter

airport

aeropuerto

tower

toren

passenger

pasahero

container

container

carton

caha di carton

cart

garoshi

basket

macutu

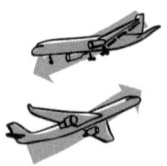

take off / land

lanta / baha

city

ciudad

village

pueblo

city centre

centro di ciudad

house

cas

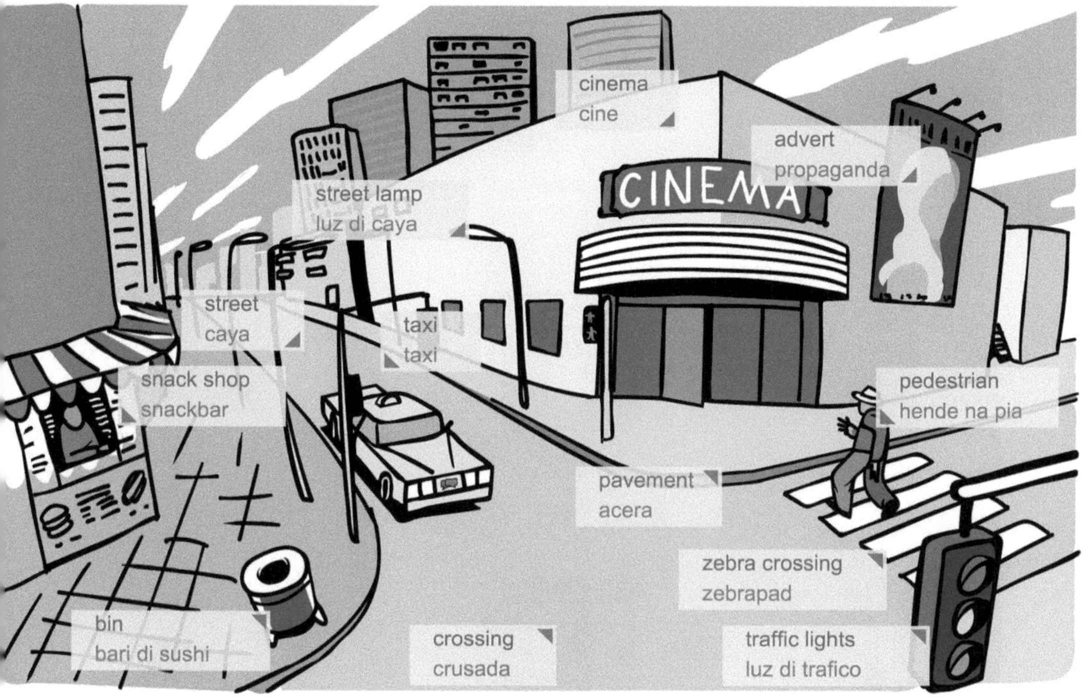

cinema
cine

advert
propaganda

street lamp
luz di caya

CINEMA

street
caya

taxi
taxi

snack shop
snackbar

pedestrian
hende na pia

pavement
acera

zebra crossing
zebrapad

bin
bari di sushi

crossing
crusada

traffic lights
luz di trafico

hut

hut

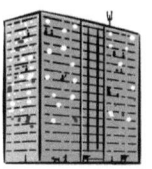

flat

flat

train station

stacion di trein

town hall

stadhuis

museum

museo

school

scol

university

universidad

bank

banco

hospital

hospital

hotel

hotel

pharmacy

botica

office

oficina

book shop

boekhandel

shop

tienda

florist's

floresteria

supermarket

supermarket

market

mercado

department store

department store

fishmonger's

bendedo di pisca

shopping centre

shopping center

harbour

haf

park

park

bench

banki

bridge

brug

stairs

trapi

underground

metro

tunnel

tunnel

bus stop

parada di bus

bar

bar

restaurant

restaurant

postbox

postbox

street sign

borchi di nomber di caya

parking meter

parkeermeter

zoo

parke di bestia

swimming pool

piscina

mosque

moskee

farm

cunucu

pollution

polucion

graveyard

santana

church

misa

playground

speelplaats

temple

tempel

landscape

paisahe

signpost
borchi di direccion

way
caminda

meadow
sabana

stone
piedra

tree
palo

hiker
keirodo

river
riu

grass
yerba

flower
flor

valley

vallei

hill

sero

lake

lago

forest

mondi

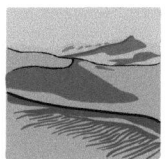

desert

desierto

volcano

volcan

castle

kasteel

rainbow

arco iris

mushroom

paddenstoel

palm tree

palma

mosquito

sangura

fly

musca

ant

vruminga

bee

bij

spider

haraña

beetle

tor

frog

dori

squirrel

eekhoorn

hedgehog

porcospina

hare

coneu

owl

shoco

bird

parha

swan

zwaan

boar

porco di mondi

deer

bina

moose

eland

dam

dam

wind turbine

molina di biento

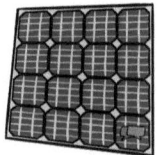

solar panel

panel solar

climate

clima

restaurant

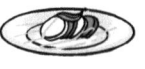

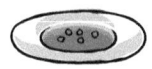

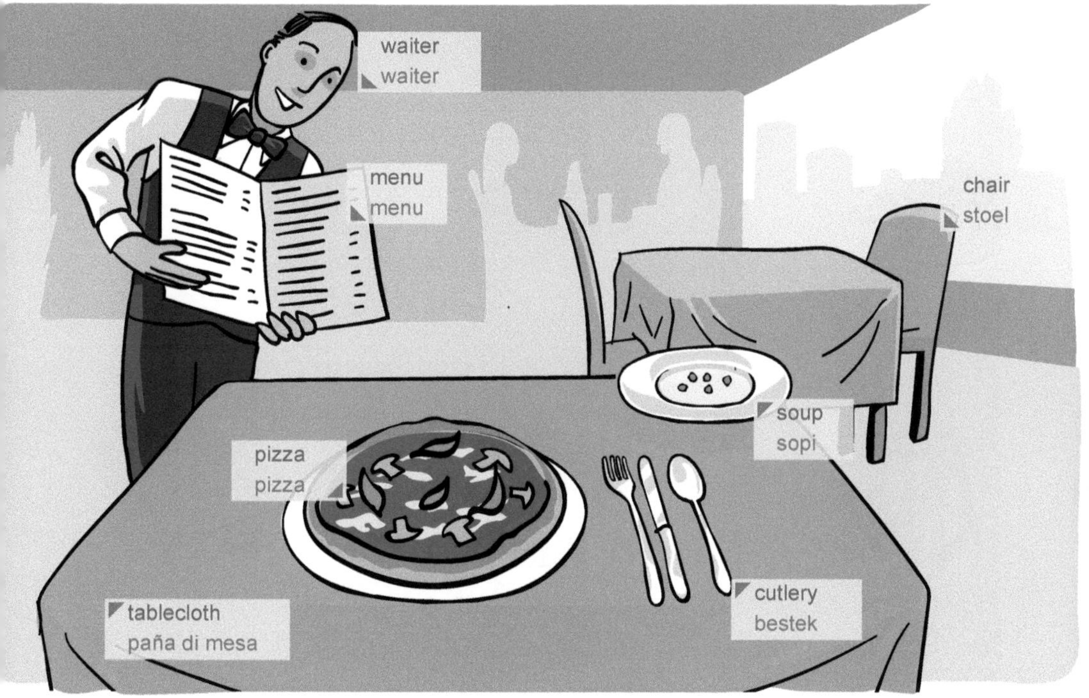

waiter
waiter
menu
menu
chair
stoel
soup
sopi
pizza
pizza
tablecloth
paña di mesa
cutlery
bestek

starter
aperitivo

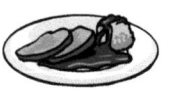

main course
cuminda principal

dessert
dessert

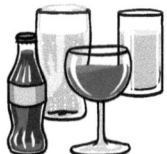

drinks
bebida

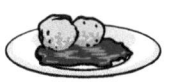

food
cuminda

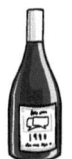

bottle
boter

fast food

fastfood

street food

streetfood

teapot

canica di te

sugar bowl

pochi di sucu

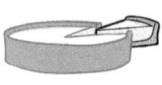

portion

porcion

espresso machine

espressomachine

high chair

stoel di mucha

bill

cuenta

tray

hasechi

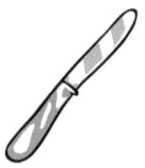

knife

cuchiu

fork

forki

spoon

cuchara

teaspoon

telep

serviette

napkin

glass

glas

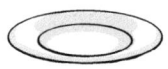

plate

tayo

soup plate

tayo di sopi

saucer

scoter

sauce

saus

salt pot

pochi di salo

pepper mill

mulina di peper

vinegar

binager

oil

azeta

spices

specerij

ketchup

ketchup

mustard

mosterd

mayonnaise

mayonaise

supermarket

supermarket

special offer
oferta special
FOR
customer
cliente
dairy
producto lacteo
fruit
fruta
trolley
garoshi di compra

BUTCHERS

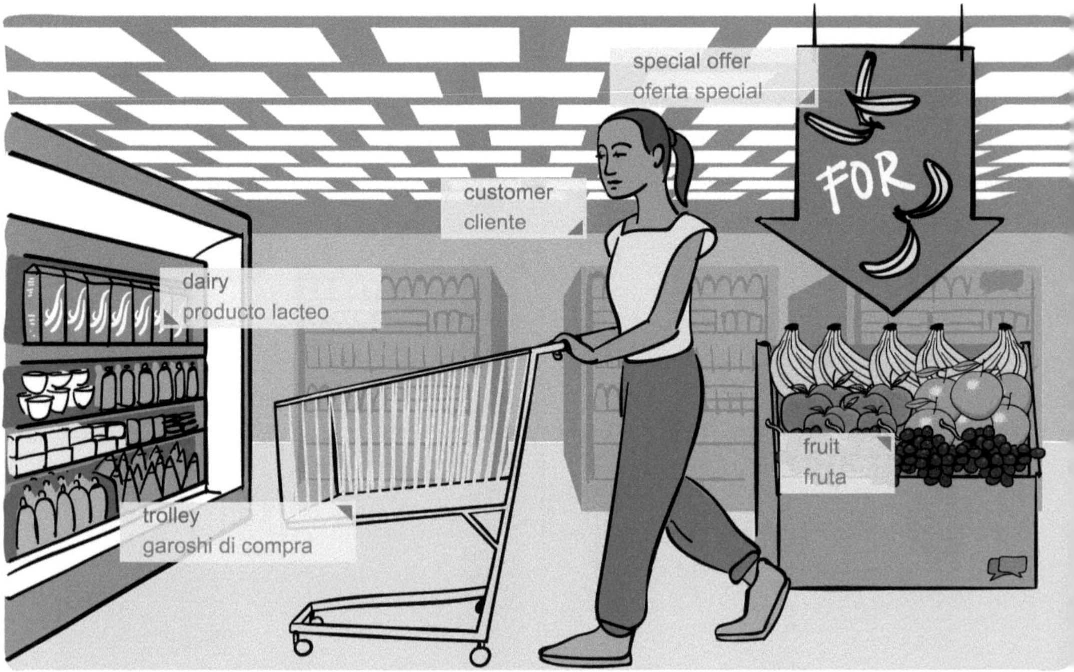

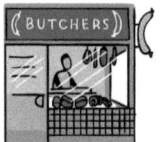

butcher´s

carniceria

BAKERY

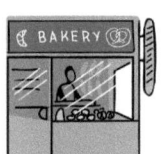

baker´s

panaderia

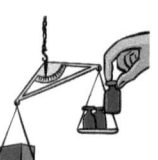

weigh

pisa

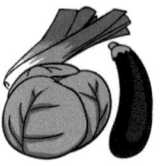

vegetables

berdura

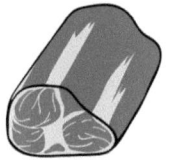

meat

carni

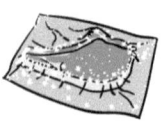

frozen food

frozen food

cold meat

beleg di carni

tinned food

cuminda di bleki

washing powder

detergente na puiro

sweets

mangel

household products

producto pa cas

cleaning products

articulo di limpiesa

salesperson

bendedo

till

cahero

cashier

cahero

shopping list

lista di compra

opening hours

orario

wallet

cartera

credit card

credit card

bag

tas

plastic bag

saco di plastic

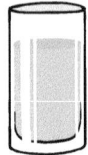

water

awa

juice

juice

milk

lechi

coke

cola

wine

biña

beer

cerbes

alcohol

alcohol

cocoa

chocomel

tea

te

coffee

koffie

espresso

espresso

cappuccino

cappuccino

banana

bacoba

apple

appel

orange

apelsina

melon

milon

lemon

lamunchi

carrot

wortel

garlic

conoflok

bamboo

bambu

onion

siboyo

mushroom

mushroom

nuts

noot

noodles

pasta

spaghetti

spaghetti

rice

aros

salad

salada

chips

batata hasa

fried potatoes

batata hasa

pizza

pizza

hamburger

hamburger

sandwich

sandwich

cutlet

cutlet

ham

ham

salami

salami

sausage

soseishi

chicken

galiña

roast

hasa

fish

pisca

porridge oats

papa

muesli

müsli

cornflakes

cornflakes

flour

hariña

croissant

croissant

bread roll

pan rondo

bread

pan

toast

toast

biscuits

cuki

butter

manteca

curd

kwark

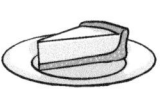

cake

bolo

egg

webo

fried egg

webo hasa

cheese

keshi

ice cream

ijscream

sugar

sucu

honey

honing

jam

jam

chocolate spread

pasta di chuculati

curry

curry

goat

cabrito

cow

baca

calf

bishe

pig

porco

piglet

yiu di porco

bull

toro

goose

gans

duck

pato

chick

puyito

hen

galiña

cock

gay

rat

djaca

cat

pushi

mouse

raton

ox

toro

dog

cacho

doghouse

cas di cacho

garden hose

slang pa muha mata

watering can

gieter

scythe

herment pa corta yerbe

plough

ploeg

sickle
garabati

hoe
chapi

pitchfork
forki pa coy hooi

axe
hacha

wheelbarrow
garetia

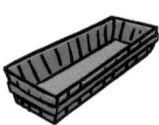

trough
pesebre

milk can
canica di lechi

sack
saco

fence
heki

stable
stal

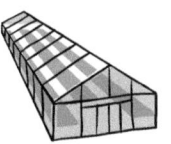

greenhouse
greenhouse

soil
suela

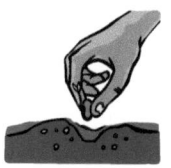

seed
simia

fertilizer
mest

combine harvester
mashin di cosecha

harvest

cosecha

harvest

cosecha

yams

yams

wheat

trigo

soy

soya

potato

batata

corn

maishi

rapeseed

canola

fruit tree

palo di fruta

cassava

yuca

cereals

grano

living room

sala

bathroom

baño

kitchen

cushina

bedroom

camber

child's room

camber di mucha

dining room

comedo

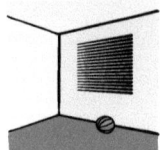

floor

suela

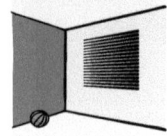

wall

muraya

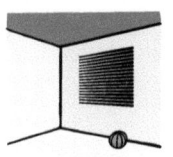

ceiling

blafon

cellar

bodega

sauna

sauna

balcony

balcon

terrace

terasa

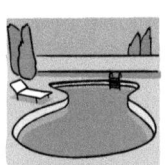

pool

piscina

lawn mower

mashin di corta yerba

sheet

laken

bedspread

bedsprei

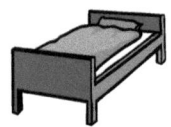

bed

cama

broom

basora

bucket

hemchi

switch

switch

living room

sala

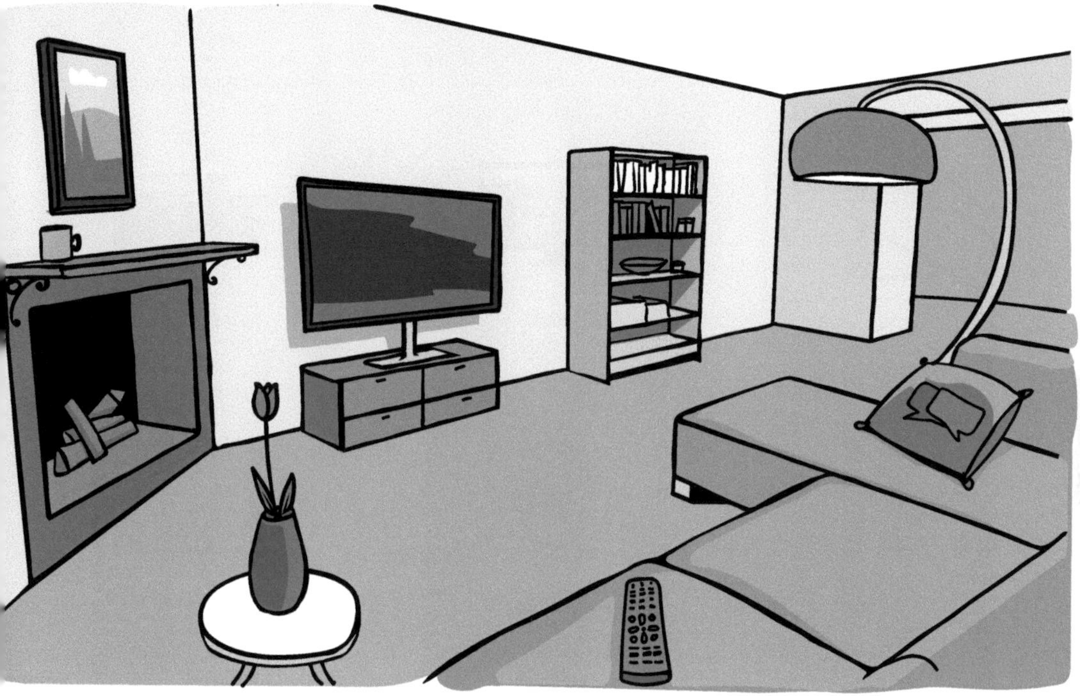

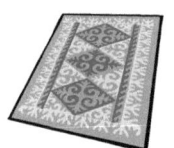

carpet

tapijt

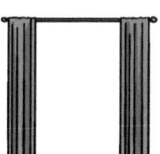

curtain

cortina

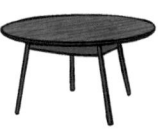

table

mesa

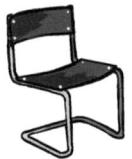

chair

stoel

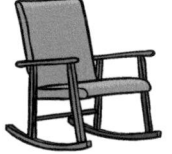

rocking chair

stoel di zoya

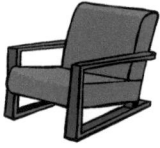

armchair

stoel

book
buki

blanket
dekel

decoration
decoracion

firewood
palo pa kima

film
film

hi-fi equipment
stereoset

key
yabi

newspaper
corant

painting
cuadra

poster
poster

radio
radio

notepad
blocnote

hoover
stofzuiger

cactus
cadushi

candle
bela

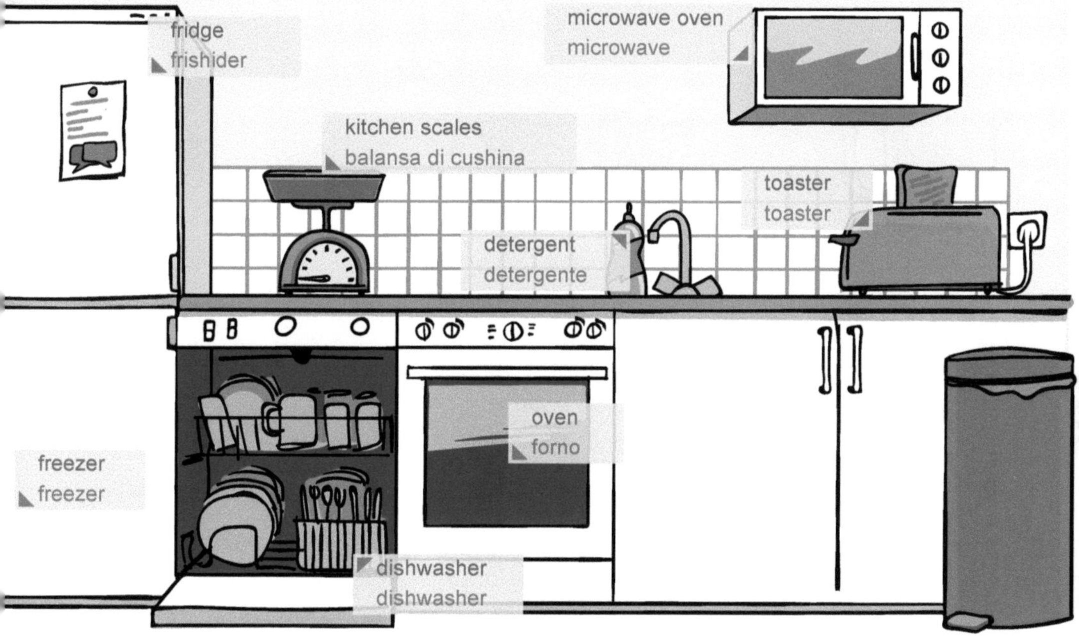

fridge
frishider

microwave oven
microwave

kitchen scales
balansa di cushina

toaster
toaster

detergent
detergente

oven
forno

freezer
freezer

dishwasher
dishwasher

cooker

stoof

pot

wea

cast-iron pot

wea di hero

wok / kadai

wok

pan

planchi

kettle

ketel

steamer

steamer

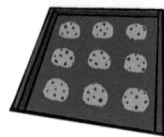

baking tray

teblachi pa horna

crockery

servies

mug

beker

bowl

conchi

chopsticks

chopstick

ladle

cuchara di sopi

spatula

spatula

whisk

garde

strainer

scurido

sieve

colado

grater

raspa

mortar

fenso

barbecue

barbecue

open fire

candela

chopping board

planki pa corta

rolling pin

rostok

corkscrew

kurkentrek

can

bleki

can opener

cos di habri bleki

pot holder

pannenlap

sink

wasbak

brush

skeiro

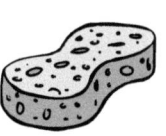

sponge

spons

blender

blender

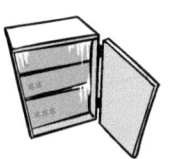

deep freezer

freezer

baby bottle

tetero

tap

cranchi

bathroom
baño

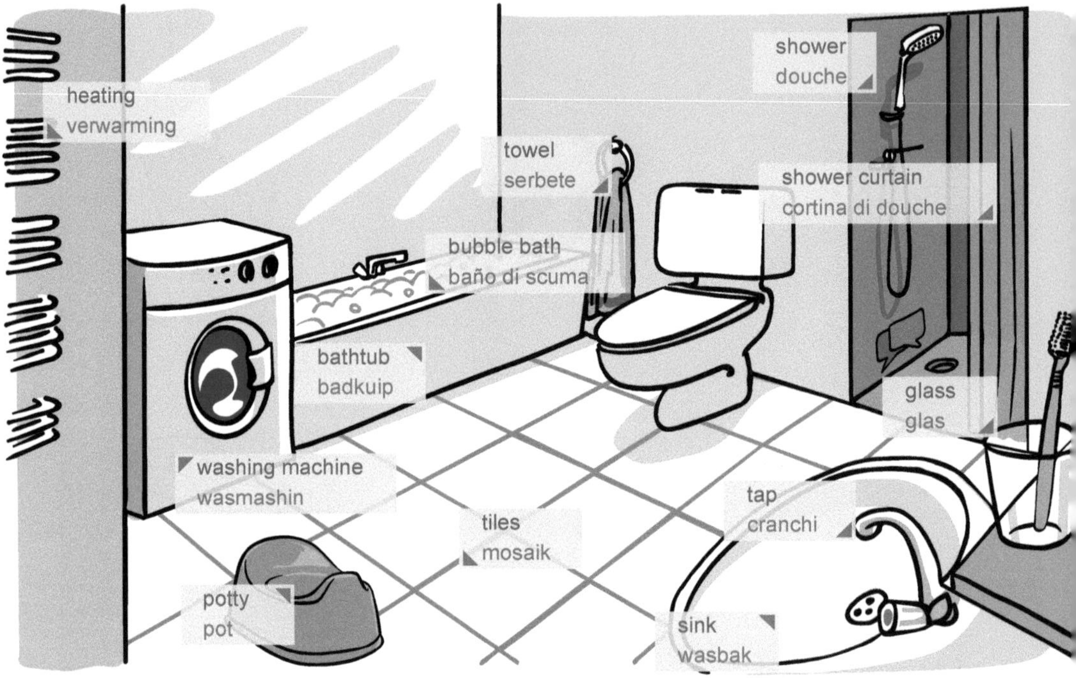

heating
verwarming
towel
serbete
shower
douche
shower curtain
cortina di douche
bubble bath
baño di scuma
bathtub
badkuip
glass
glas
washing machine
wasmashin
tap
cranchi
tiles
mosaik
potty
pot
sink
wasbak

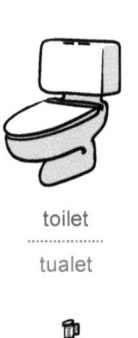

toilet

tualet

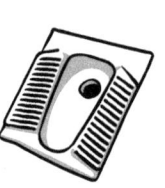

squat toilet

hurktoilet

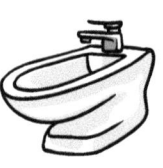

bidet

bidet

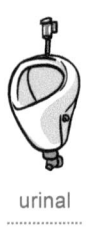

urinal

urinal

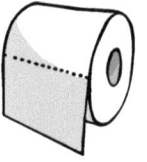

toilet paper

papel di w.c.

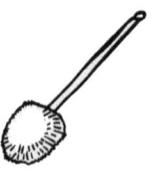

toilet brush

skeiro di w.c.

toothbrush

skeiro di djente

toothpaste

pasta di djente

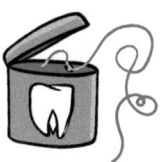

dental floss

dental floss

wash

laba

handheld shower

douche di man

douche

bidet

basin

tobo

back brush

skeiro

soap

habon

shower gel

shower gel

shampoo

shampoo

flannel

washandje

drain

drain

cream

crema

deodorant

desodorante

mirror

spiel

hand mirror

spiel di man

razor

blet

shaving foam

shaving foam

aftershave

aftershave

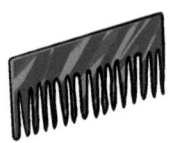

comb

peña

brush

skeiro

hair dryer

blower

hairspray

spray pa cabey

makeup

makeup

lipstick

lipstick

nail varnish

cos di pinta huña

cotton wool

catuna

nail scissors

sker pa corta huña

perfume

perfume

washbag

tas

stool

kruk

weighing scale

balansa

bathrobe

bata

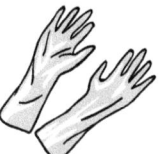

rubber gloves

handschoen

tampon

tampon

sanitary towel

kotex

chemical toilet

wc kimico

child's room

camber di mucha

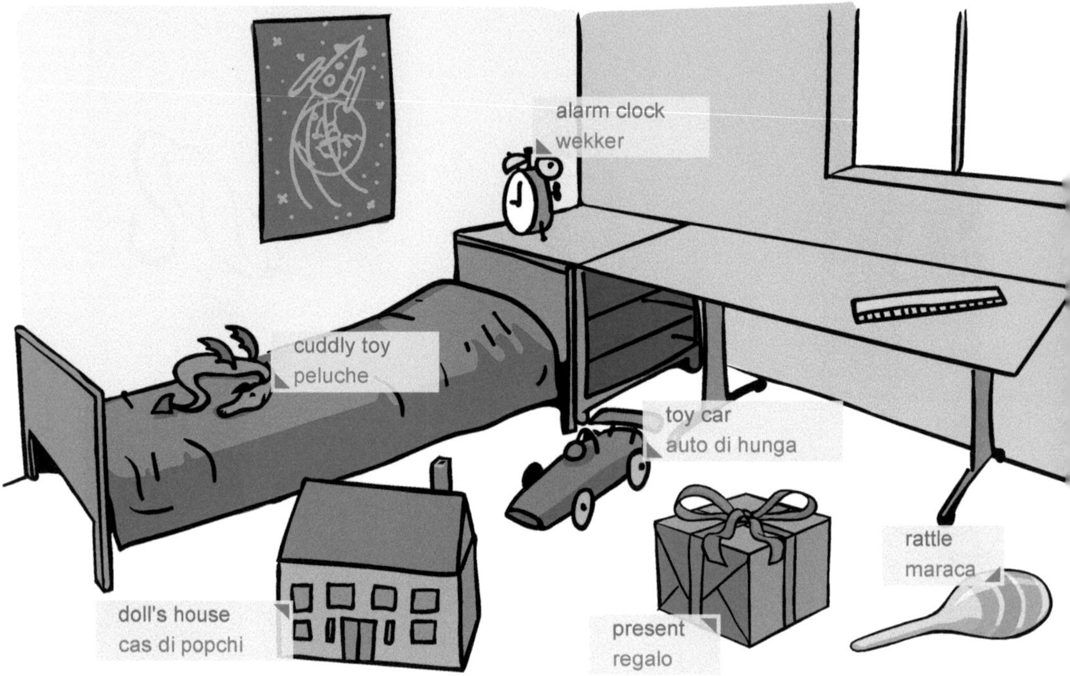

alarm clock
wekker
cuddly toy
peluche
toy car
auto di hunga
rattle
maraca
doll's house
cas di popchi
present
regalo

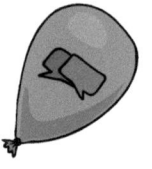

balloon

blaas

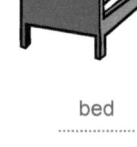

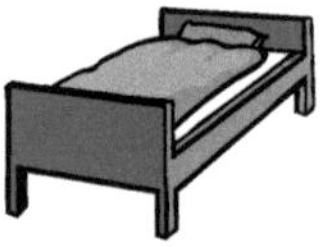

bed

cama

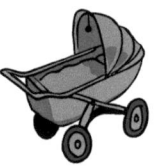

pram

stroller

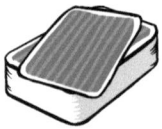

deck of cards

baraha di carta

jigsaw

puzzel

SUPER
MEGA

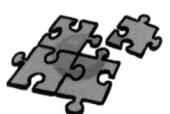

comic

comic

lego bricks

lego

building blocks

bloki di hunga

action figure

figura di accion

babygrow

romper

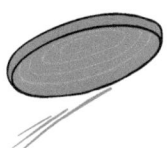

frisbee

frisbee

mobile

mobil

board game

wega di mesa

dice

dou

model train set

set di trein

dummy

chupon

party

fiesta

picture book

buki di prenchi

ball

bala

doll

popchi

play

hunga

sandpit

zandbak

swing

zoya

toys

cos di hunga

video game console

videogame

tricycle

tricycle

teddy bear

beer

wardrobe

cashi di paña

clothing

paña

socks

mea

stockings

mea

tights

pantyhose

scarf
sjaal

belt
faha

umbrella
paraplu

t-shirt
T-shirt

trainers
keds

boots
boots

slippers
slof

sandals
sandalia

shoes
sapato

rubber boots
laars di rubber

underpants
carsonsio

bra
bh

vest
flanel

clothing - paña

body

body

trousers

carson

jeans

jeans

skirt

saya

blouse

blusa

shirt

camisa

pullover

sweater

hoodie

sweater

blazer

blazer

jacket

jacket

coat

jas

raincoat

regenjas

costume

flus

dress

shimis

wedding dress

shimis di bruid

suit

flus

nightgown

yapon

pyjamas

pidjama

sari

sari

headscarf

lenso di cabes

turban

turban

burqa

burqa

kaftan

kaftan

abaya

abaya

swimsuit

zwempak

trunks

zwembroek

shorts

carson cortico

tracksuit

trainingspak

apron

lantera

gloves

handschoen

button

boton

glasses

bril

bracelet

armband

necklace

cadena

ring

renchi

earring

renchi di horea

cap

pechi

coat hanger

kapstok

hat

sombre

tie

dashi

zip

ziper

helmet

helm

braces

guiel

school uniform

uniform di scol

uniform

uniform

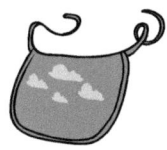

bib

babado

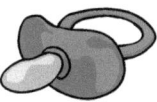

dummy

chupon

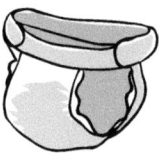

nappy

bruki

office

oficina

server
server
filing cabinet
filekast
printer
printer
paper
papel
monitor
pantaya
mouse
mouse
desk
lessenaar
folder
map
keyboard
keyboard
waste-paper basket
bari di sushi
chair
stoel
computer
computer

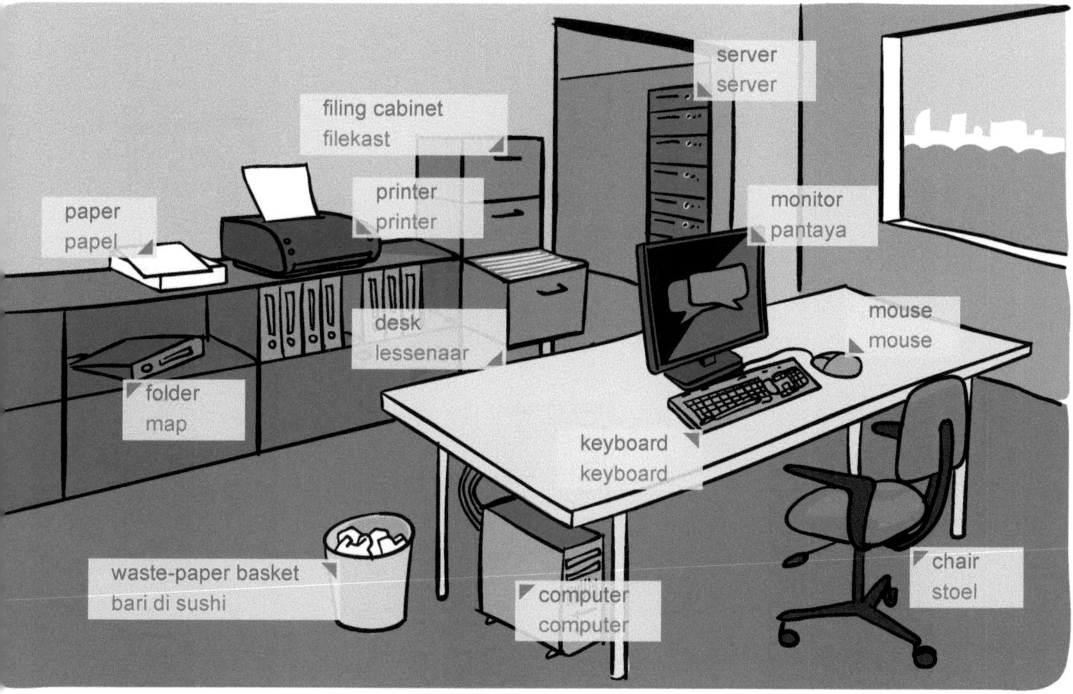

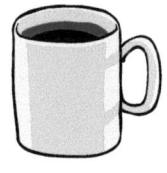

coffee mug

copi pa bebe koffie

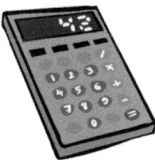

calculator

calculator

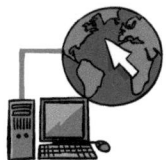

internet

internet

laptop

laptop

letter

carta

message

mensahe

mobile

celular

network

red

photocopier

mashin di copia

software

software

telephone

telefon

plug socket

stopcontact

fax machine

fax mashin

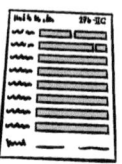

form

formulario

document

documento

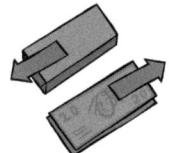

buy

cumpra

pay

paga

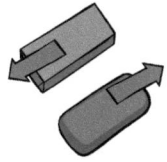

trade

negosha

money

placa

dollar

dollar

euro

euro

yen

yen

rouble

roebel

Swiss franc

frank suiso

renminbi yuan

yuan renminbi

rupee

roepi

cashpoint

bancomatico

bureau de change

oficina di cambio

gold

oro

silver

plata

oil

azeta

energy

energia

price

prijs

contract

contract

tax

impuesto

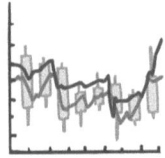

stock

share

work

traha

employee

empleado

employer

dunado di trabou

factory

fabrica

shop

tienda

occupations
ofishi / profesion

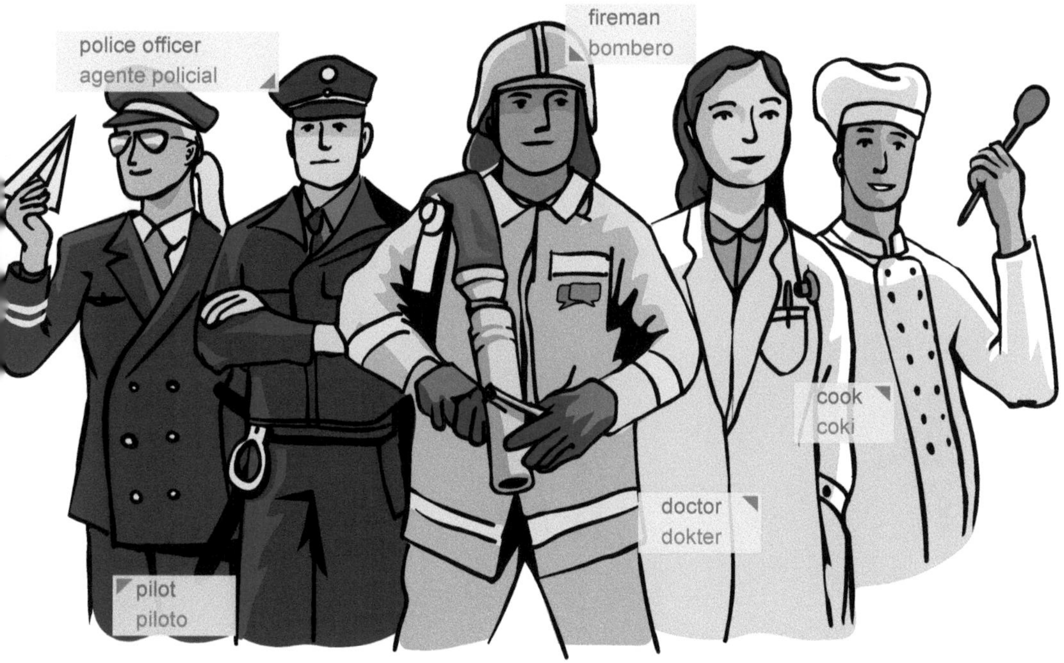
police officer
agente policial
fireman
bombero
cook
coki
doctor
dokter
pilot
piloto

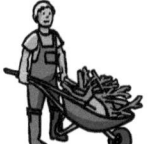

gardener

hardinero

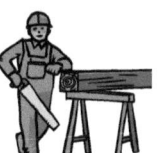

carpenter

carpinte

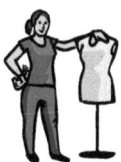

seamstress

cosedo

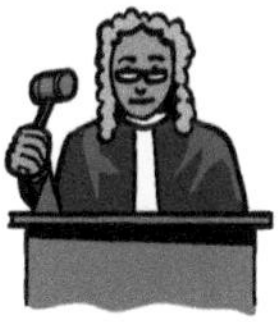

judge

hues

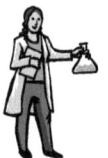

chemist

kimico

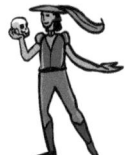

actor

actor

bus driver

chauffeur di bus

taxi driver

chauffeur di taxi

fisherman

piscado

cleaning lady

hende cu ta haci cas limpi

roofer

drechado di dak

waiter

waiter

hunter

jaagdo

painter

verfdo

baker

panadero

electrician

electricista

builder

trahado den construccion

engineer

ingeniero

butcher

carnicero

plumber

loodgieter

postman

partido di carta

soldier

solda

architect

arkitecto

cashier

cahero

florist

florista

hairdresser

pelukero / pelukera

conductor

controlado di ticket

mechanic

mecanico

captain

capitan

dentist

dentista

scientist

cientifico

rabbi

rabbi

imam

imam

monk

monk

clergyman

pastor

tools
herment

pliers
pins
hammer
martiu
screwdriver
schroefdraai
torch
flashlight
spanner
wrench

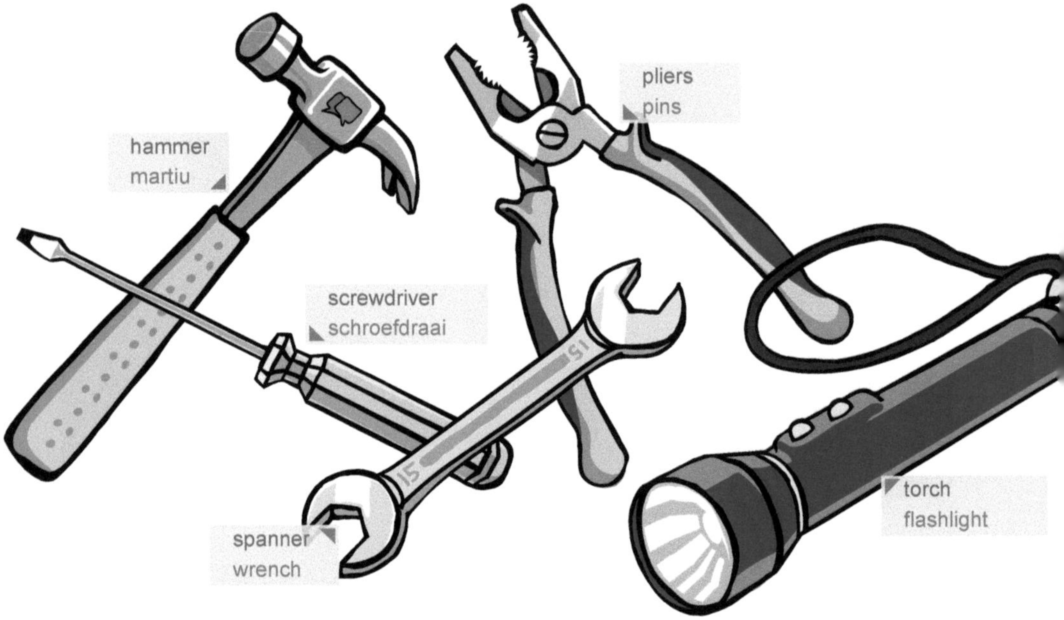

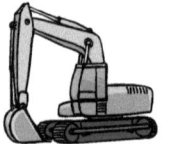

digger
bulldozer

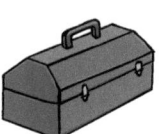

toolbox
caha di herment

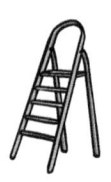

ladder
trapi

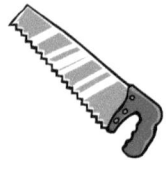

saw
zaag

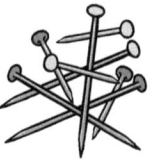

nails
clabo

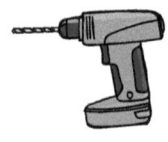

drill
boormashin

repair
drecha

shovel
shobel

Damn!
caraho!

dustpan
scop

paint pot
bleki di verf

screws
schroef

musical instruments
instrumento musical

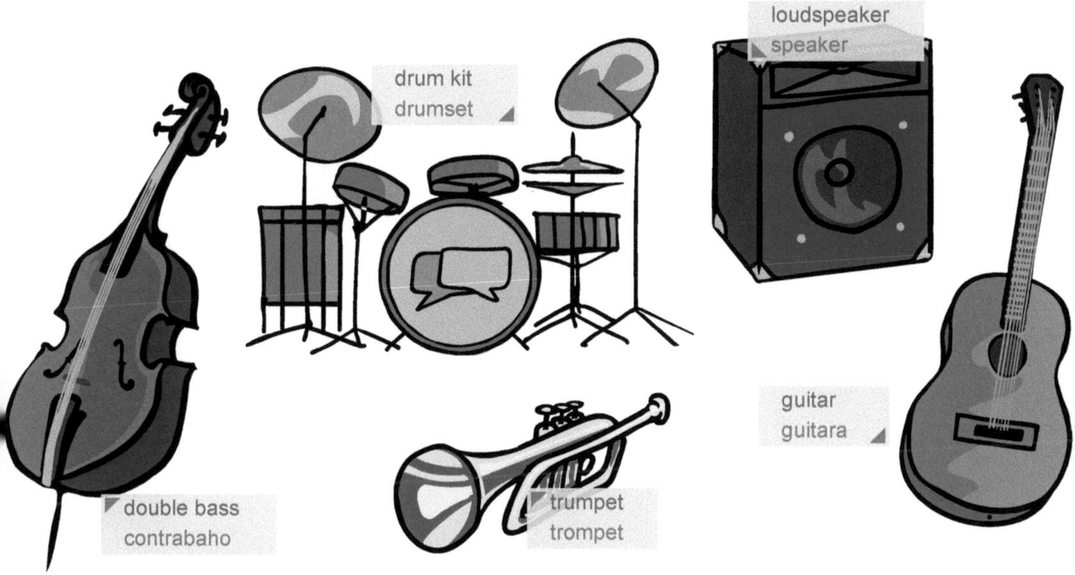

drum kit
drumset

loudspeaker
speaker

guitar
guitara

double bass
contrabaho

trumpet
trompet

piano

piano

violin

fio

bass

baho

timpani

timbal

drums

tambu

keyboard

keyboard

saxophone

saxofon

flute

fluit

microphone

microfon

zoo

parke di bestia

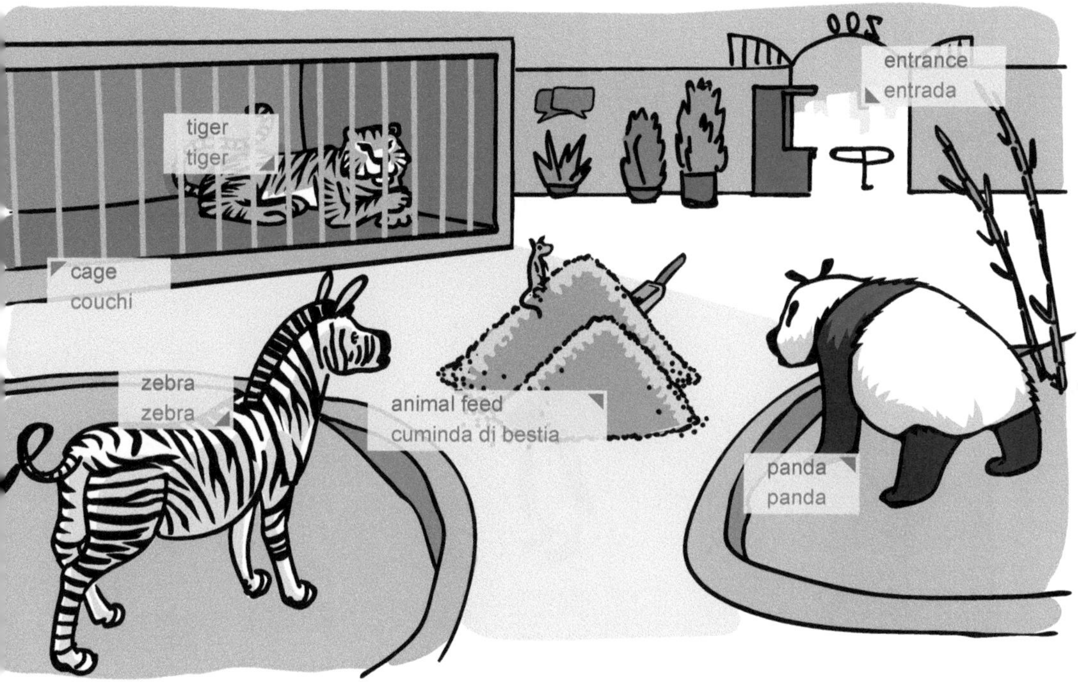

tiger
tiger
cage
couchi
zebra
zebra
animal feed
cuminda di bestia
panda
panda
entrance
entrada

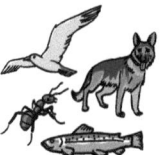

animals

animal

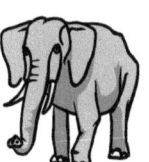

elephant

olifante

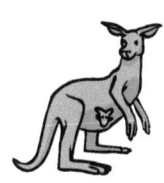

kangaroo

cangaru

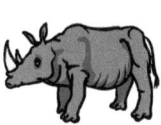

rhino

neushoorn

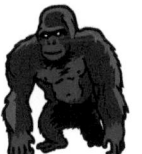

gorilla

gorila

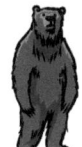

bear

beer

camel

camel

ostrich

avestruz

lion

leon

monkey

macaco

flamingo

flamingo

parrot

lora

polar bear

beer polar

penguin

pinguin

shark

tribon

peacock

pauwies

snake

colebra

crocodile

caiman

zookeeper

cuidado di bestia

seal

cacho di awa

jaguar

jaguar

pony

pony

leopard

leopardo

hippo

hipopotamo

giraffe

giraf

eagle

aguila

boar

porco di mondi

fish

pisca

turtle

turtuga

walrus

walrus

fox

vos

gazelle

gazelle

American football
futbol Americano

cycling
ciclismo

tennis
tennis

basketball
basketball

swimming
landamento

boxing
boxeo

ice hockey
ice hockey

football
······
futbol

badminton
······
badminton

athletics
······
atletismo

handball
······
handbal

skiing
······
ski

polo
······
polo

jump
bula

laugh
hari

hug
brasa

walk
cana

sing
canta

dream
soña

pray
resa

kiss
sunchi

write skirbi	draw pinta	show mustra
push primi	give duna	take coy

have
tin

do
haci

be
ta

stand
para

run
core

pull
ranca

throw
tira

fall
cay

lie
drumi

wait
warda

carry
carga

sit
sinta

get dressed
bisti

sleep
drumi

wake up
lanta fo'i soño

look at

mira

cry

yora

stroke

caricia

comb

peña

talk

papia

understand

compronde

ask

puntra

listen

scucha

drink

bebe

eat

come

tidy up

ruim op

love

stima

cook

cushna

drive

bai

fly

bula

activities - actividad

sail

zeilo

calculate

conta

read

lesa

learn

siña

work

traha

marry

casa

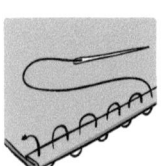

sew

cose

brush teeth

skeiro djente

kill

mata

smoke

huma

send

manda

family
famia

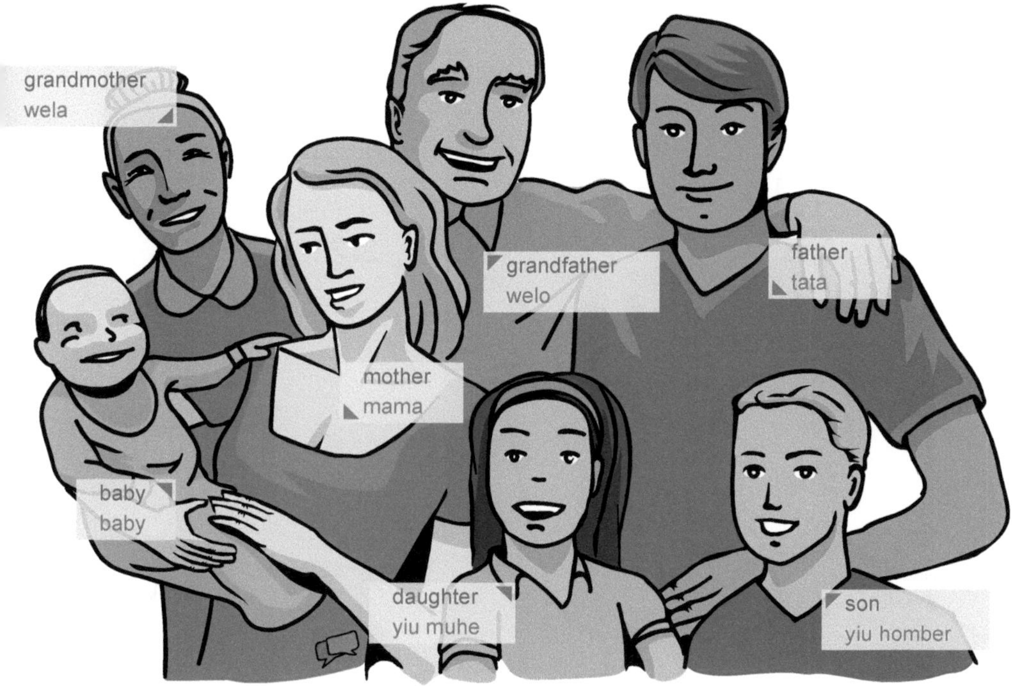

grandmother
wela
grandfather
welo
father
tata
mother
mama
baby
baby
daughter
yiu muhe
son
yiu homber

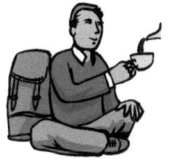

guest
huesped

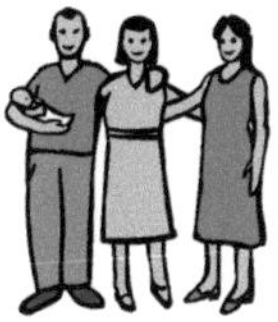

aunt
tanta

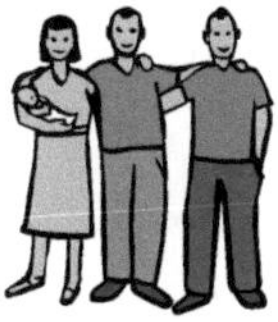

uncle
omo

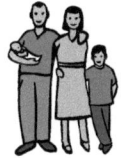

brother
ruman homber

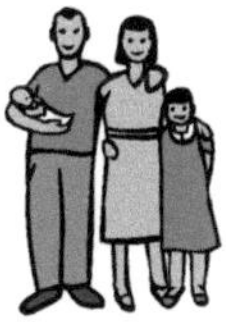

sister
ruman muhe

body

curpa

forehead
frenta
eye
wowo
shoulder
schouder
finger
dede
face
cara
chin
cachete
hand
man
breast
pecho
leg
pia
arm
brasa

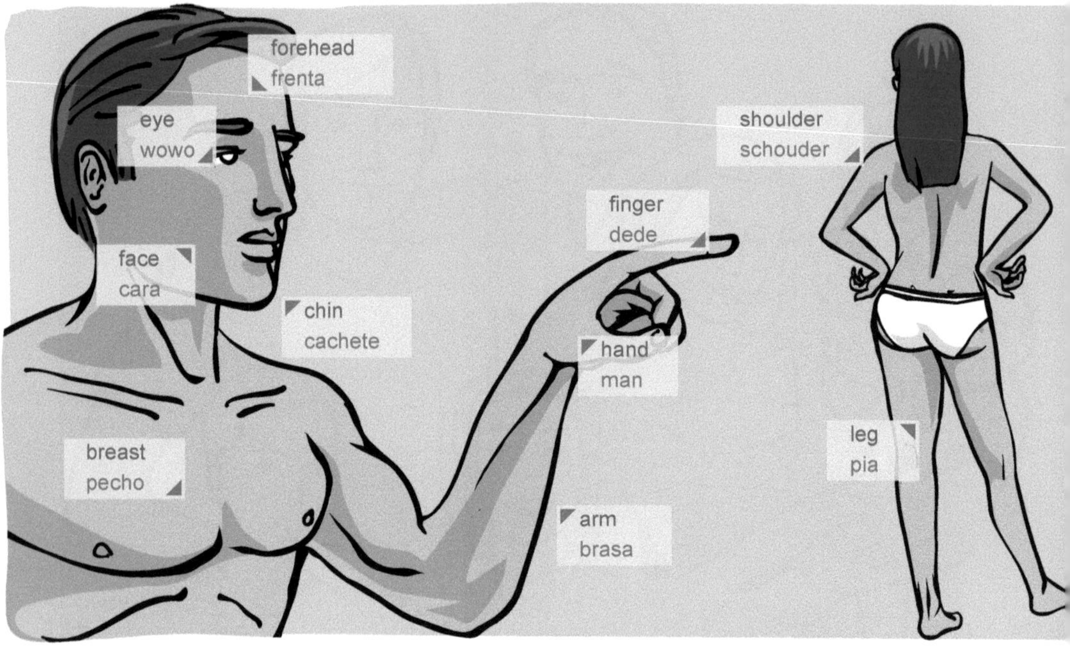

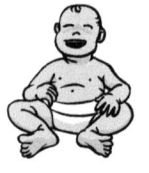

baby

baby

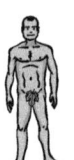

man

homber

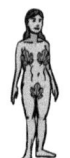

woman

muhe

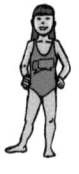

girl

mucha muhe

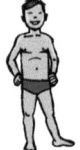

boy

mucha homber

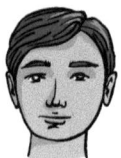

head

cabes

back

lomba

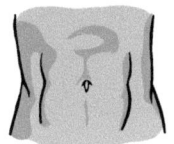

belly

bariga

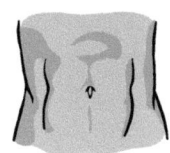

belly button

lombrishi

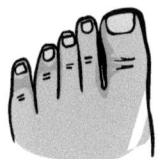

toe

dede di pia

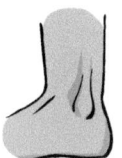

heel

hilchi

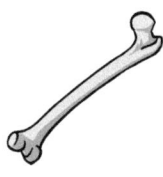

bone

weso

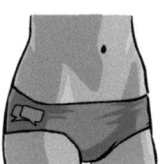

hip

heup

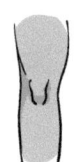

knee

rudia

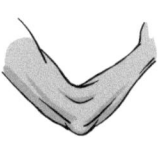

elbow

elleboog

nose

nanishi

bottom

chanchan

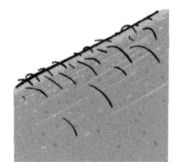

skin

cuero

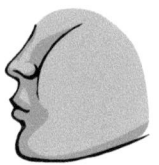

cheek

wang

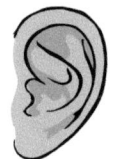

ear

horea

lip

lip

mouth

boca

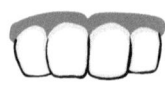

tooth

djente

tongue

lenga

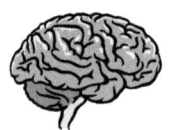

brain

celebro

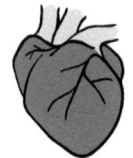

heart

curason

muscle

musculo

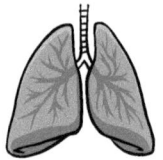

lung

pulmon

liver

higra

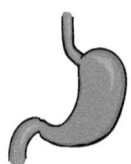

stomach

stoma

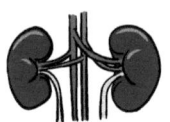

kidneys

nier

sex

sex

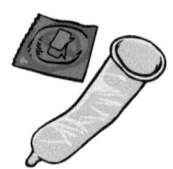

condom

condon

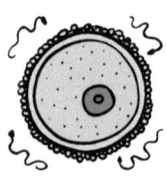

ovum

ovulo

semen

sperma

pregnancy

embaraso

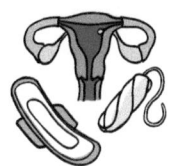

menstruation

menstruacion

vagina

vagina

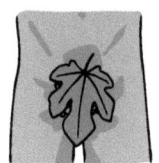

penis

penis

eyebrow

wenkbrauw

hair

cabey

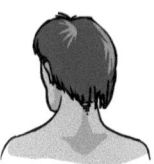

neck

nek

hospital
hospital

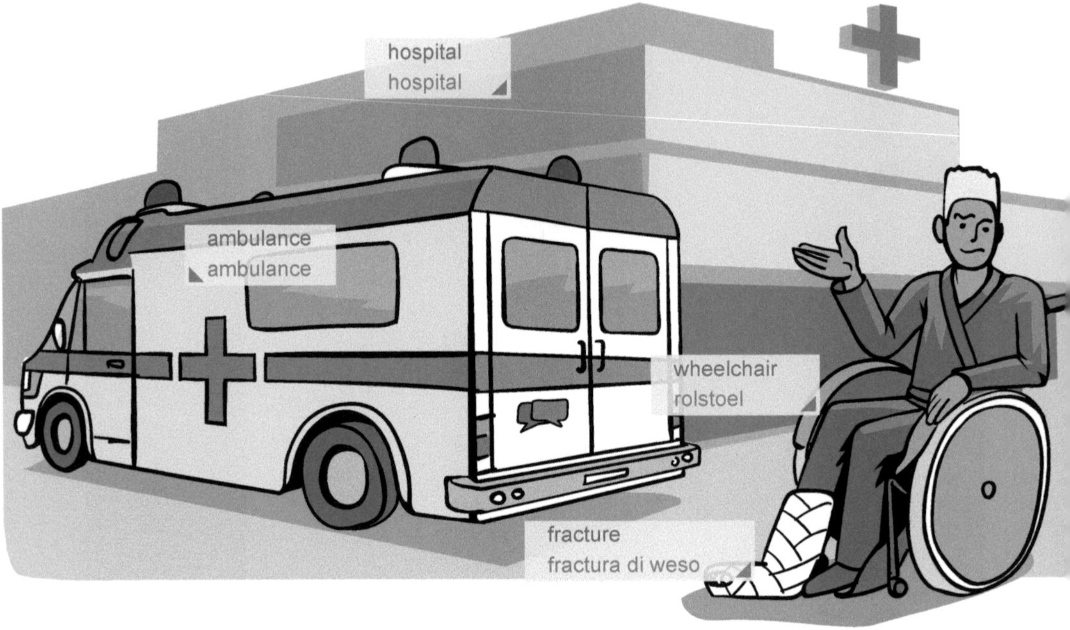

hospital
hospital
ambulance
ambulance
wheelchair
rolstoel
fracture
fractura di weso

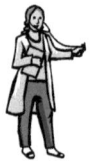

doctor

dokter

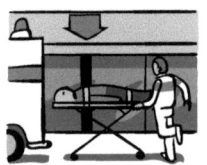

emergency room

EHBO (prome asistencia/eerste hulp)

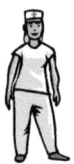

nurse

nurse

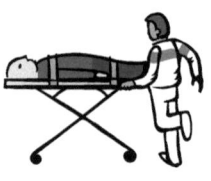

emergency

caso di emergencia

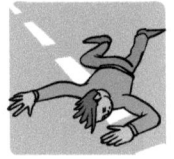

unconscious

fo'i tino

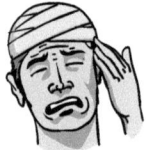

pain

dolor

injury

lesion

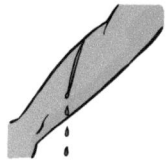

bleeding

sangramento

heart attack

ataca di curason

stroke

ataca celebral

allergy

alergia

cough

tosa

fever

keintura

flu

griep

diarrhoea

diarea

headache

dolor di cabes

cancer

cancer

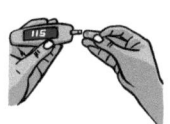

diabetes

diabetes

surgeon

ciruhano

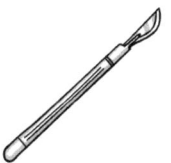

scalpel

scalpel

operation

operacion

CT

CT

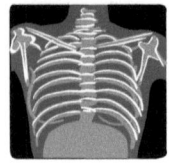

x-ray

x-ray

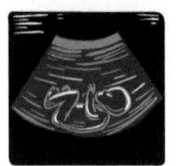

ultrasound

echo

face mask

masker contra stof

disease

malesa

waiting room

sala di espera

crutch

kruk

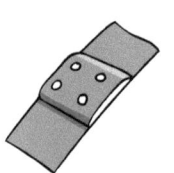

plaster

pleister

bandage

verband

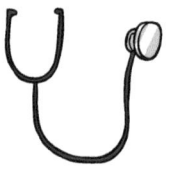

injection

inyeccion

stethoscope

stetoscop

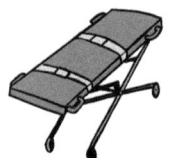

stretcher

brancard

clinical thermometer

thermometer

birth

nacemento

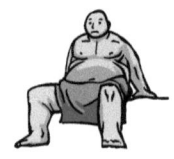

overweight

sobrepeso

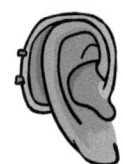

hearing aid

aparato pa oido

disinfectant

desinfectante

infection

infeccion

virus

virus

HIV / AIDS

HIV / AIDS

medicine

remedi

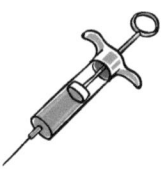

vaccination

vacuna

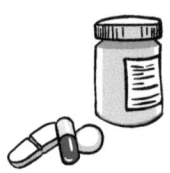

tablets

pilder

pill

pilder

emergency call

yamada di emergencia

blood pressure monitor

aparato pa midi presion

ill / healthy

malo / saludabel

Help!	alarm	assault
auxilio!	alarma	atraco

attack	danger	emergency exit
atake	peliger	salida di emergencia

Fire!	fire extinguisher	accident
candela	brandspuit	desgracia

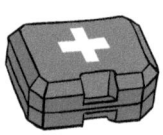

first-aid kit	SOS	police
caha di prome asistencia	SOS	polis

Europe

Europa

North America

Noord America

South America

Sur America

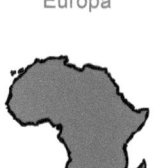

Africa

Africa

Asia

Asia

Australia

Australia

Atlantic

Oceano Atlantico

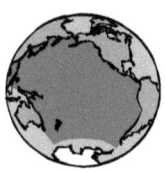

Pacific

Oceano Pacifico

Indian Ocean

Oceano Indio

Antarctic Ocean

Oceano Antartico

Arctic Ocean

Oceano Artico

North Pole

Noordpool

South Pole

Zuidpool

Antarctica

Antartica

Earth

mundo

land

tera

sea

lama

island

isla

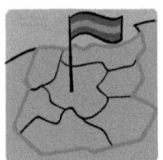

nation

nacion

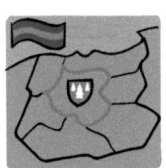

state

estado

clock face

holoshi analog

hour hand

wijzer chikito

minute hand

wijzer grandi

second hand

wijzer di seconde

What time is it?

Cuant'or tin?

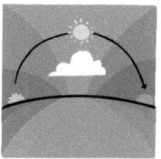

day

dia

time

tempo

now

awor

digital watch

holoshi digital

minute

minuut

hour

ora

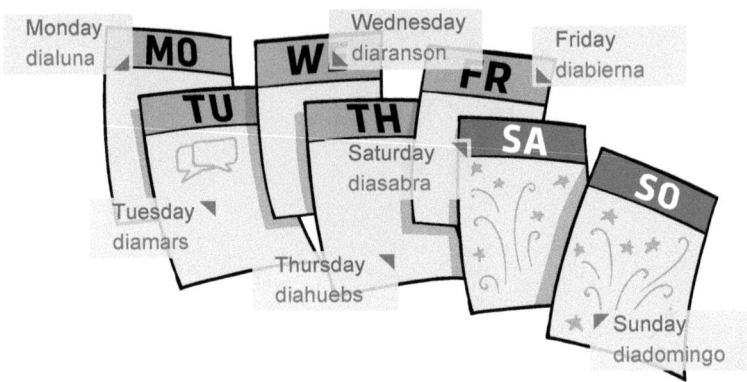

Monday
dialuna

Wednesday
diaranson

Friday
diabierna

Tuesday
diamars

Saturday
diasabra

Thursday
diahuebs

Sunday
diadomingo

yesterday

ayera

today

awe

tomorrow

mañan

morning

mainta

noon

merdia

evening

anochi

MO	TU	WE	TH	FR	SA	SU
1	2	3	4	5	6	7
8	9	10	11	12	13	14
15	16	17	18	19	20	21
22	23	24	25	26	27	28
29	30	31	1	2	3	4

business days

dia di trabou

MO	TU	WE	TH	FR	SA	SU
1	2	3	4	5	6	7
8	9	10	11	12	13	14
15	16	17	18	19	20	21
22	23	24	25	26	27	28
29	30	31	1	2	3	4

weekend

weekend

year

aña

rain
awacero
spring
lente
summer
zomer
wind
biento
autumn
herfst
snow
sneeuw
winter
winter

4.APRIL 11°
5.APRIL 4°
6.APRIL 13°
7.APRIL 8°
8.APRIL 10°

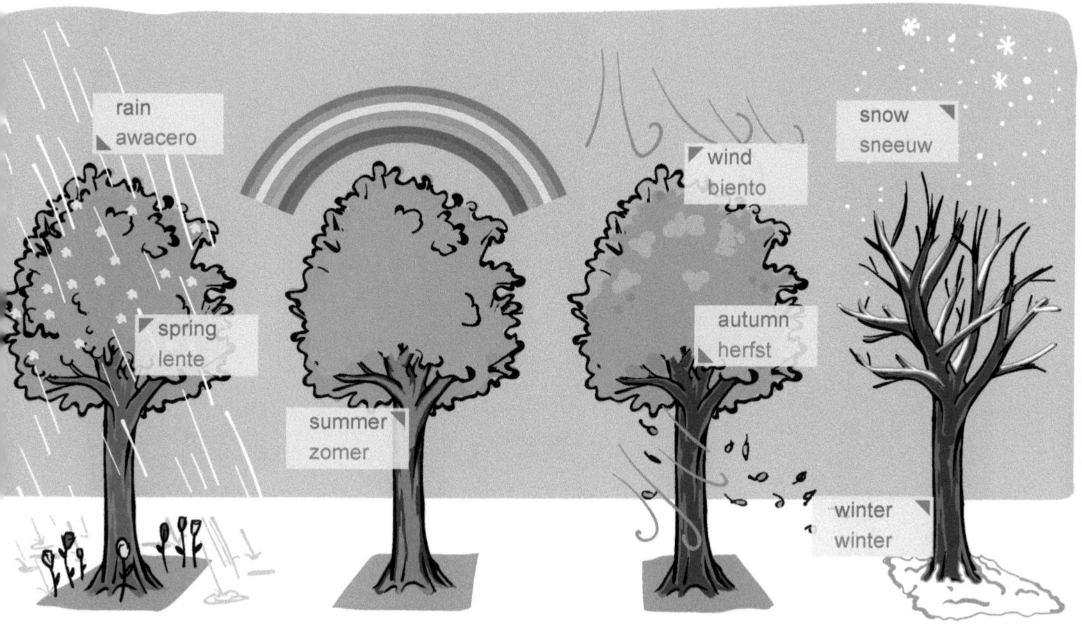

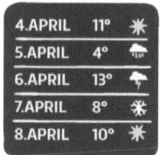

weather forecast

pronostico di tempo

F C
120 40
90 30
60 20
30 10
0 0
-30 -10
-20

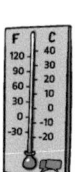

thermometer

thermometer

sunshine

solo ta briya

cloud

nubia

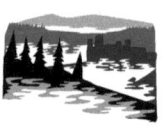

fog

neblina

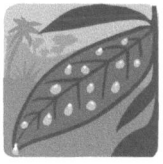

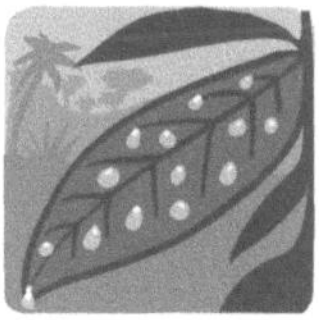

humidity

humedad

lightning

lamper

thunder

strena

storm

mal tempo

hail

hagel

monsoon

mal tempo

flood

inundacion

ice

ijs

January

januari

February

februari

March

maart

April

april

May

mei

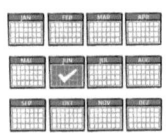

June

juni

July

juli

August

augustus

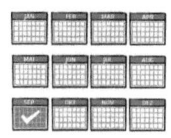

September
september

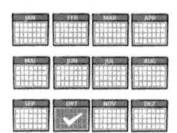

October
october

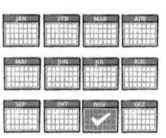

November
november

December
december

shapes
forma

circle
circulo

square
cuadra

rectangle
rectangulo

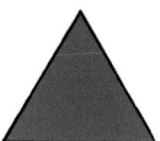

triangle
triangulo

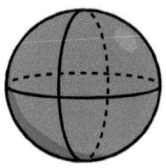

sphere
bol

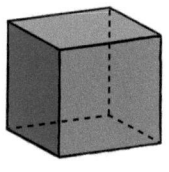

cube
kubus

white

blanco

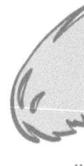

yellow

geel

orange

oraño

pink

ros

red

cora

purple

biña

blue

blauw

green

berde

brown

bruin

grey

shinishi

black

preto

a lot / a little

hopi / tiki

angry / calm

rabia / trankil

beautiful / ugly

bunita / mahos

beginning / end

comienso / final

big / small

grandi / chikito

bright / dark

cla / scur

brother / sister

ruman homber / ruman muhe

clean / dirty

limpi / sushi

complete / incomplete

completo / incompleto

day / night

dia / anochi

dead / alive

morto / bibo

wide / narrow

hancho / smal

edible / inedible

comibel / incomibel

evil / kind

mal hende / bon hende

excited / bored

ansioso / ferfela bo mes

fat / thin

gordo / flaco

first / last

prome / ultimo

friend / enemy

amigo / enemigo

full / empty

yen / bashi

hard / soft

duro / moli

heavy / light

pisa / lihe

hunger / thirst

hamber / sed

ill / healthy

malo / saludabel

illegal / legal

ilegal / legal

intelligent / stupid

inteligente / sabi

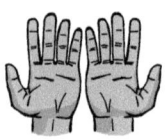

left / right

robes / drechi

near / far

cerca / leu

new / used

nobo / uza

nothing / something

nada / algo

old / young

bieu / jong

on / off

cendi / paga

open / closed

habri / cera

quiet / loud

keto / duro

rich / poor

rico / pober

right / wrong

bon / fout

rough / smooth

grof / liso

sad / happy

tristo / contento

short / long

cortico / largo

slow / fast

pocopoco / lihe

wet / dry

muha / seco

warm / cool

cayente / friu

war / peace

guera / paz

opposites - contrario

numbers

cifra

0

zero

cero

1

one

un

2

two

dos

3

three

tres

4

four

cuater

5

five

cinco

6

six

seis

7

seven

shete

8

eight

ocho

9

nine

nuebe

10

ten

dies

11

eleven

diesun

12

twelve

diesdos

13

thirteen

diestres

14

fourteen

diescuatro

15

fifteen

diescinco

16

sixteen

diesseis

17

seventeen

diesshete

18

eighteen

diesocho

19

nineteen

diesnuebe

20

twenty

binti

100

hundred

shen

1.000

thousand

mil

1.000.000

million

miyon

English

Ingles

American English

Ingles Mericano

Chinese Mandarin

Chines Mandarin

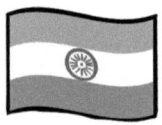

Hindi

Hindi

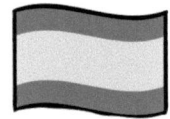

Spanish

Spaño

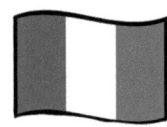

French

Frances

Arabic

Arabe

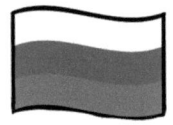

Russian

Ruso

Portuguese

Portugues

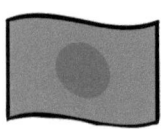

Bengali

Bengal

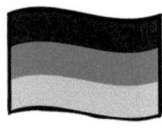

German

Aleman

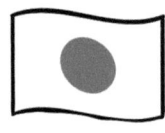

Japanese

Hapones

I

ami

you

abo

he / she / it

e

we

nos

you

boso

they

nan

who?

ken?

what?

kico?

how?

con?

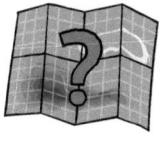

where?

unda?

when?

ki ora?

name

nomber

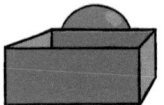

behind

patras

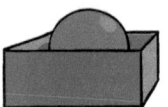

in

den

in front of

dilanti di

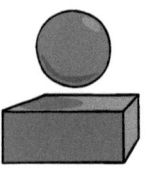

over

ariba

on

riba

under

bou di

beside

banda di

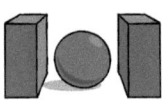

between

entre

place

luga